How to Give A Party

PARTIES

How To Give A Party

A FIRST BOOK

by Jean and Paul Frame

illustrated by Paul Frame

FRANKLIN WATTS, INC.
New York
1972

Cover design by Nick Krenitsky

SBN 531-00759-6
Copyright © 1972 by Franklin Watts, Inc.
Library of Congress Catalog Card Number: 74-183296
Printed in the United States of America
6 5 4 3 2 1

Contents

1

Basic Rules and First Plans

Anyone can give a party. There are, however, a few basic rules to follow that will help to make *your* party one to remember.

Giving a party can be a bucket of laughs, with some work thrown in to make sure that the fun keeps coming. Or a party can be a great deal of work and pretty much of a drag. If there were a magic formula for a great party, it would have to be *plan well*.

First things first: choose your planners. In most cases, this will probably be your mother and you. But there's no law that says it can't be you and your father or another relative or maybe a good friend, one with ideas and one who doesn't turn pale when there's work to be done. This is really one of the best parts of party-giving. Planning and working out details with your family or friends, and sometimes both, can be as much fun as the party itself.

Once you have decided whom you want to ask, make the date far enough in the future so you will have plenty of time to work out the arrangements — at least two or three weeks is a good idea. This also gives everyone enough time so they can be sure to have the date free.

The reason your guest list is almost the first thing you work on is that the people you invite often give you an idea of the games to play and what the theme will be. A party of all girls or all boys, for example, can be very different from a party of boys and girls together.

It is a good idea to have a party theme — this helps you to choose the kind of decorations you want. Besides making food ideas come more easily, a party theme always seems to strike a good starting note for the party.

A smoothly run party is the party that guests will remember with pleasure. There are several ways of making sure of this. One, you can work your planner to a frazzle. Two, do a lot of hosting or hostessing yourself. And three, invite a responsible friend. He or she can help run the games, hold down the noise if necessary, and give a hand with the refreshments.

If you're old enough to help plan a party, you're old enough to help with every part of it. Working at hospitality really isn't work at all. It is making people want to come to your home again.

There is a most important suggestion to remember in planning a good party. *Keep things moving.* Start the party as soon as the first three or four guests arrive. To make sure that none of your plans get lost in the excitement, have your ideas written down — a list of games to play, when to start them, and about what time you plan to serve the food. This way you have a handy reminder that keeps the party from slowing down or getting out-of-hand.

Below is a suggested outline for your party plans. You may find it helpful to write the outline on a large sheet of paper with additions of your own. As you go along with your plans, you can check off the items after you complete each one — write notes to yourself as reminders and, in general, keep tabs on your party plans. Give yourself a complete "state-of-my-party" file all during the planning. In this way, you make sure that you don't discover, as the guests arrive, that you've forgotten to get the pencils you need for the Telegram game or the mustard for the frankfurters.

Party Plans

A. Who will plan with you?
   1. mother
   2. other relative
   3. friend
B. Party list
   1. how many
   2. who
   3. be sure everyone gets along
C. Invitations
   1. by phone
   2. buy
   3. make
D. Helping hands
   1. older brother or sister
   2. parent
   3. friend
E. Keep party moving
   1. games for the "early birds"
   2. action games
   3. quiet in-between games to keep the "lid on"
   4. prizes (if you choose)
F. Food
   1. plan menu to please guests and your budget
   2. plan menu according to party theme
G. Decorations
   1. according to party theme
      a. indoor — remove all furniture possible
      b. outdoor — hope for clear skies
   2. supplies you need to buy

3

2

Decorating Hints

Perhaps the most important thing in making your own decorations is planning what you want so you will know what materials you need. List them, and find out where you can get them for little or no money — for instance, old paper or wooden boxes from your grocer. Start your plans early enough so you'll have ample time to collect your supplies.

Painting your decorations: Usually poster paints are the best to use and the most flexible — also, happily, the least expensive. Basic colors can be mixed to get a wider range of tones. Experiment. For example, black and red in equal parts produce brown; add white and you get pinkish brown; add yellow and you get a warmer brown. Test to discover the amounts you need for the shades you want. The clerk in your local art-supply store can also tell you what colors to mix to get a wide variety of shades.

Brushes: The best all-around size is a ¼-inch chisel-end brush. However, you may find that you work better with other sizes or one with more of a point. This is something you'll have to discover by using various sizes. You might get several inexpensive sizes and shapes. Try them out and see which works best for you.

If you find that you can't make paint stay on a smooth or waxy surface, such as a balloon or oilcloth or milk carton, mix the paint with pure liquid soap. You will find that soap should do the trick.

Supplies: If you intend to do much "making" of things, always have spool wire on hand. Keep Scotch tape handy, too, for it has unending uses in making things. There is also a tape made with adhesive on both sides, called double-stick tape. This is great in making hidden seams. (*See Basic Skills, Skill 3*)

Learn how useful old mailing tubes or the cardboard tube centers used in many paper products, such as paper towels, can be.

If you become a real do-it-yourself buff, there are many good books, probably in your local library, that can be most helpful. Also, two magazines, *Woman's Day* and *Family Circle,* usually found in your local chain food store, often carry good "how-to" articles. Get in the habit of saving the articles that interest you.

For things to make out of paper and cardboard, ask your librarian for a book called *Paper Playtime* by Sadami Yamada. It has a number of things to make and gives patterns to follow. Also, it will give you ideas on how to design many of your own animals.

House & Garden, Better Homes & Gardens, and other national magazines usually publish entire issues at Christmastime on how to make many wonderful gifts. They offer party suggestions that could be used all year round.

When the directions for making a party decoration seem unclear, use a newspaper to experiment with, rather than trying it first with the finished material.

Keep a party box. In it store all the supplies you will need to start any party. Also store the things you see in-between parties that you think might be good for a future gathering: how-to articles in magazines, bits and pieces of colored paper that can be used in games or decorations, even invitation ideas. This can become a good way to keep down your expenses, and it is very convenient to have a lot of working materials around just to get your imagination started.

3

Lists and Invitations

The very first item of party business is to decide whom you are going to ask, and how and when you will ask them. While making your list, keep in mind the first rule of a good guest list. Each person should get along with all the other guests. One sour note caused by a "feud" can change a good party into a sad happening.

Don't make your list too long. A very large party tends to need a lot of skilled help to keep the big crowd from falling into small, separate groups. More than one skilled person to help, besides you and your mother, can be hard to find. Don't invite more guests than you and your planners can handle. Don't complicate what is supposed to be a wonderful, relaxing time for all.

Remember: give yourself and your guests as much notice as possible before the big day.

There are two ways of inviting guests: by telephone or by written invitation. (If you see everybody in school, of course, you could invite them in person.)

Probably the quickest way is the telephone. Before you start the first call, jot down a list of the important details, so that you don't hang up without mentioning the time or date. And, of course, if you are planning a special kind of party, you should mention anything out of the ordinary that you might want your guests to know about. If the party is to be outdoors, with very active games, for example, falls or stains are a good bet, so you should add "no dress up" clothes to your list of information.

If you decide on written invitations, you have two choices — buying them or making them. Stationery stores and variety stores sell attractive invitations with blank spaces for filling in the time, place, date, and whatever else your guests need to know. There is usually a large selection of invitations, so it is just a matter of finding the one that fits your kind of party. Remember, if you are inviting someone you don't often see or someone who no longer lives near you, it is wise to include clear directions on how to reach your home. You wouldn't want a friend to arrive two hours after the

party is over. This sort of oversight can put a considerable strain on the best of friendships, no matter whose fault it was. But nobody ever lost a party or a friend by planning well and thoughtfully.

Making your own invitations can be fun. It can also save money. And even more important, they can be tailored to your own particular party. Everyone will see that you cared enough about your party to take the time to make each invitation.

Here are some suggestions for making your own.

One of the simplest ways is to use a tracing (see *Basic Skills, Skill 1*) of your favorite comic-strip character to decorate the outside. Taking any notepaper as your starting point, let the size of your decoration determine the size of your invitation. Try not to go over 5 by 7 inches. This size can be folded with the outside showing your decoration and perhaps a line such as "Hope you're not too busy" or "Please save (day and date)." On the inside right-hand flap, put the time and place. If it is to be a special party, tell what the theme is: birthday, holiday, and so on. On the left-hand side, add any special information, such as "Wear old clothes; we're going to make things."

You may want to use something other than a cartoon or comic character on your invitations. If so, keep this in mind as you look through magazines. If you see something attractive or amusing that you might use in the future, cut it out and put it in your party box.

You can also use colored construction paper that you can buy in any variety store. To design your own invitations, you are limited only by what you feel would be too complicated — and your own imagination.

If you have no special theme in mind, but still want an attractive invitation of your own design, get an old seed catalog and cut out the pictures you like the best. Then paste them on the front of the invitations.

4

Party Themes

A central idea — a party theme — can be a great help. It can help you in deciding everything you plan for your party, from invitations, decorations, and menus, right through to what games to play.

If you and your planner feel that making your own decorations is too much work, many stores carry party kits. Each usually consists of a centerpiece for the refreshment table that sets the theme — perhaps a paper Halloween pumpkin — and a matching tablecloth, napkins, cups, plates, candy baskets, and sometimes favors.

If you enjoy making things, choose one of the themes on the following pages. The suggestions on how you can "put-the-party-together" with what you make are easy to follow.

The party plans are intended for both indoors and out, on a specific theme. However, with a change here and there, the basic ideas and some decorations can be used for an "anywhere-anytime-of-the-year" party. Just remember that the first sit-down planning session will be very important. That is when you decide what you can afford to buy, beg, or borrow to make the party go.

Always plan on paper plates, cups, and napkins. In the long run they save money (they don't break), and they also, of course, eliminate the chore of washing dishes! If the party is indoors, clear the area of breakables and as much furniture as is practical.

If you plan well, and everyone uses his imagination fully, you will have a party that should be fun from the first thought to the good-byes at the end. And although no one is going to tell you that cleaning up is fun, there are three basic rules — applicable to almost any kind of party — to make it easier: (1) As far as possible, use things that can be thrown away, (2) have cardboard cartons available for refuse, and (3) have on hand sponges or paper towels to cope with accidents.

The following suggestions and directions should help to solve most of your problems, with one major exception — the budget. Your family may be willing to pay the party expenses, but once you know how much you'll need, you might also work at odd jobs for your relatives or neighbors. Actually, it's a very good feeling to be able to finance a party through your own efforts.

Balloon Party

Most parties are simply excellent excuses for getting together to have fun in gay and colorful surroundings. So, what could be better than a Balloon Party!

This is party for anytime of the year. You needn't wait for a special occasion. Best of all, you don't need a lot of money.

Supplies

(Supplies such as scissors, glue, rulers, or pencils, which you will need for making practically all decorations, are not listed.)
balloons, all colors
compass or 3 round objects of different diameters, or see *Basic Skills, Skill 2*

construction paper, various colors that go well with your basic color
   scheme, and green for tree leaves
crepe paper, 3 or more colors, one of which should be green
double-stick tape
masking tape
newspapers
pliers
roasting pan or basket
spool wire
string, medium weight
wastebaskets (2)
wire hangers (11 or more)

Your color scheme for the Balloon Party can be any gay combination of two (or more) colors. You can, if your budget allows, use clusters of balloons wherever your eye decides you need color. If money is a problem, you can cut flat balloons from colored construction paper.

For decorations on and around your front door, you can use all or parts of the ideas shown in Sketch 1. (Balloon Party sketches are on page 13.)

In Sketch 1, the decorations for the door (1A) are balloon shapes cut from colored construction paper. After cutting, attach a piece of string to each "balloon," make a large crepe-paper bow, then assemble as shown. Use double-stick tape to hold the "balloon" in place.

Two wastebaskets (1B), covered with contrasting strips of crepe paper fastened in back with tape, can be used for the "pots" to hold the balloon trees.

For each balloon tree (1C), you'll need the following supplies:

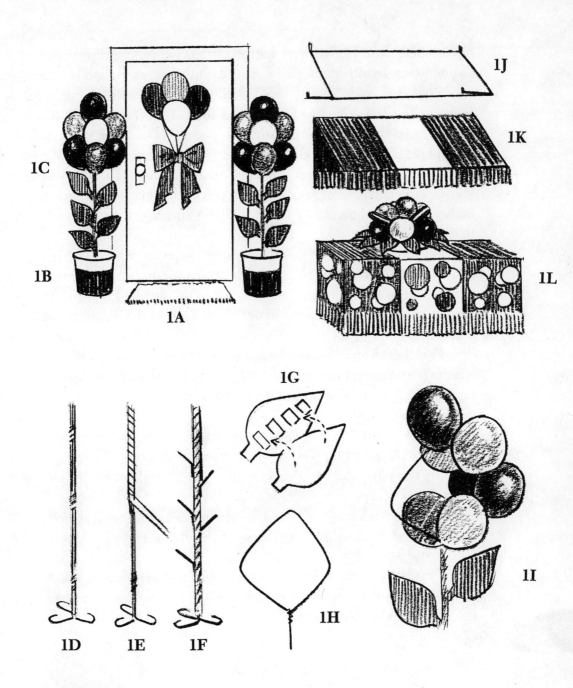

1J

1K

1C

1B

1A

1L

1G

1D 1E 1F 1H 1I

SKETCH I

newspapers, four or five wire hangers, masking tape, green crepe paper, green construction paper, string, and thirteen balloons.

First, for each "tree trunk," straighten three wire hangers, bending the last 4 inches to use as a foot (1D). Tape the three straightened hangers together in three places (1D). Cut a sheet of newspaper into 2-inch-wide strips and wind the strips around the wires to give strength and thickness to the trunk (1E). To hold leaves, cut six pieces of spool wire or a wire hanger, each piece 8 inches long. Bend back 2 inches of the wire and tape the short ends to the trunk (1F).

Cut the leaves from green construction paper, one leaf from each 8- by 10-inch sheet. Use double-stick tape to put two leaves together (1G) for each finished leaf. Tape the finished leaf to the wire stem. Wind green crepe-paper strips around the entire trunk and stems.

For the treetop, straighten the hook part of another wire hanger with pliers, bending the hanger into the shape to hold balloons (1H). Insert the straightened end into the trunk top, and tape securely.

Inflate twenty-six balloons, thirteen for each tree. Tie them in pairs as in 1I, except for the top of the tree where you will use only one. Tie the pairs close to the wire stems to keep them from dangling down.

Place balloon trees in pots. Use several heavy stones or bricks over the feet to hold the trees upright. Stuff the rest of the pots with newspaper.

To make the frame for the canopy over the refreshment table, use three or more wire hangers, depending on how long you want the canopy to be. Straighten the hangers, then bend two as shown in the solid lines (1J). To cover this, use two colors of crepe paper (1K), leaving the last 4 inches to be cut into a fringe (see *Basic Skills, Skill 8*).

For the table centerpiece (1L) use a large roasting pan, or a basket, if you have one. If you use a pan, cover it with crepe paper. Take variously shaped colored balloons, inflate, tie them with short pieces of string, and tape them into the pan or basket. Cut enough leaves to make a border. Insert the leaves around the lip of the pan or basket.

Use crepe paper for the tablecloth (1L). Alternate colors as shown. To join various colors of paper use the hidden seam method (see *Basic Skills, Skill 3*). Fringe the last 4 inches of each strip. To decorate the cloth, cut balloon shapes in various sizes and colors from construction paper. Apply as shown with double-stick tape.

Balloon Party Menu

Chop Suey on Rice

Grape Clusters   Soft Drinks   Fortune Cookies

OR

Cold Meat Platter   Potato Salad

Rolls Celery Carrots Radishes Olives Tiny Tomatoes

Lemon Sherbet   Soft Drinks   Cookies

OR

Refreshments for Afternoon Parties

Peach Ice Cream   Brownies   Soft Drinks   Candy

15

Chop Suey

1½ pounds beef, diced
¼ cup oil
2 tablespoons soy sauce
2 teaspoons salt
Freshly ground black pepper
3 cups celery, cut in 1-inch
   pieces

2 large onions, chopped
1 tablespoon molasses
2 cups beef bouillon
2 cups canned bean sprouts,
   drained
3 tablespoons cornstarch
6 cups hot cooked rice

Fry beef in oil over high heat for 3 minutes, stirring constantly. Stir in soy sauce, salt, and pepper. Remove meat from pan and keep hot. To oil remaining in saucepan, add celery, onions, molasses, and bouillon. Bring to a boil and cook for 10 minutes, stirring frequently. Add bean sprouts and cook for 3 minutes. Replace beef. Mix cornstarch and ¼ cup water, and add. Cook until thickened, stirring constantly. Serve with rice. Serves 6.

Birthday Party

The decorations for birthday parties, which may come at any time of the year, of course, are rather general in theme. Just try to make your party decorations gay and colorful. The first thing to decide is the color scheme, and then carry it throughout your party area.

Supplies

balloons, long and round shapes
construction paper, 3 colors to match crepe paper
crepe paper, 3 colors

double-stick tape
favors for each guest
hatbox or box of similar size
masking tape
ribbon
string, medium weight
tissue paper

For the front door, make a cluster of balloons, all colors. Make the string for each balloon fairly short. Every third balloon should have a different string length so that they will cluster well. To make the cluster, use double-stick tape on the backs of the balloons to keep them in place. For suggestions see 2A, 2B, and 2C in Sketch 2. (Birthday Party sketches are on page 18.)

Whether inside your house or apartment, or out-of-doors, the party area can be surrounded by clusters of balloons — real ones or colored paper ones, whichever your budget permits.

If the party is inside, the party table can, of course, be your regular dining table. If the party is outside, either of the suggestions for the Western Frontier Days Party (page 60) would do well.

In decorating the party table, use crepe paper in two of the colors you have chosen. Cut into 5-inch wide strips, then alternate the two colors as in 2D. Cut the strips so that they reach from the top of the table to the floor, with enough left over so each strip can be taped to the tabletop. Cover the top by alternating the colors in 10-inch wide strips. Dress the edge with one of your color choices. Cut a 5-inch wide strip that will reach around the table, and flute one edge (see *Basic Skills, Skill 12*).

The centerpiece (2E) is a variation of a Jack Horner Pie. Get an old hatbox or some other box about the same size. If it has no

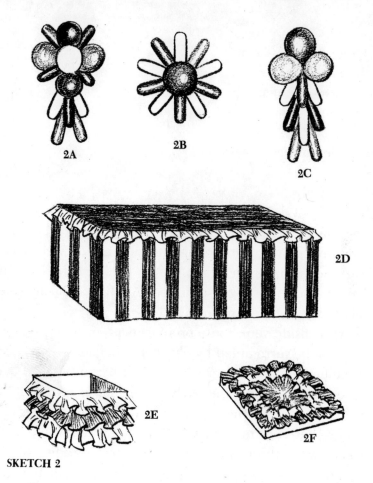

2A

2B

2C

2D

2E

2F

SKETCH 2

top, it will be necessary to make one. Cover the sides of the box with tiers of crepe paper. Cover the top with three squares of crepe paper (2F). The first square is 1 inch larger than the size of the top; the second square is 2 inches smaller than the first; and the third square is 2 inches smaller than the second. Flute the edges. Glue each layer into place, leaving the last two-thirds of each square free. Place a cluster of balloons in the shape of a flower in the center.

A nice idea is to purchase a simple favor for each guest, wrap

18

it in tissue paper, and tie it in ribbon with a long streamer. Place these favors inside the Jack Horner Pie, with the streamers spread out on the table and the lid on the box. At some point have each guest take one ribbon (while you gently lift the lid) and pull his favor out of the box.

Don't forget to decorate the trash boxes for paper plates, empties, and so forth. Covered with crepe paper and decorated with paper balloons, they will encourage your guests not to be litterbugs.

Birthday Party Menu

Fruit Salad   Crescent Roll Sandwiches
Radishes   Carrot Curls   Olives
Punch   Birthday Cake

OR

Tomato Stuffed with Cottage Cheese
Corn-bread Wedges   Celery and Carrot Sticks
Soft Drinks   Birthday Cake

OR

Refreshments for Afternoon Parties

Ice Cream   Birthday Cake
Lemonade

Crescent Roll Sandwiches

Spread refrigerated crescent rolls with grated cheese. Roll and bake as directed. Serves 8.

Circus Party

Supplies

balloons
construction paper
crepe paper (2 colors)
cup hook
favors, if desired
hatbox or box of similar size
knitting wool, red
masking tape
poster paints, red and black
spool wire
string, medium weight
tagboard

It is impractical to try to design decorations for every kind of house or apartment. So, all the suggestions in this book might require some imagination on your part. As an example, look at the illustration on the first page of this book.

For the broad stripes, alternate two colors of crepe paper. For an apartment door, each strip can be attached on the outside of the door with just a few pieces of tape here and there because there is no wind to disturb it. To do this on the outside of a house in midwinter might be more of a headache than it's worth. In that case, just do the balloon-tree idea mentioned for the Balloon Party. For other front-door decorations, see Sketch 3. (All Circus Party sketches are on pages 21 and 23.) To enlarge these sketches, see *Basic Skills, Skill 4*. Cover the center portion of the door with two panels of brightly colored crepe paper before you tape on your drawing.

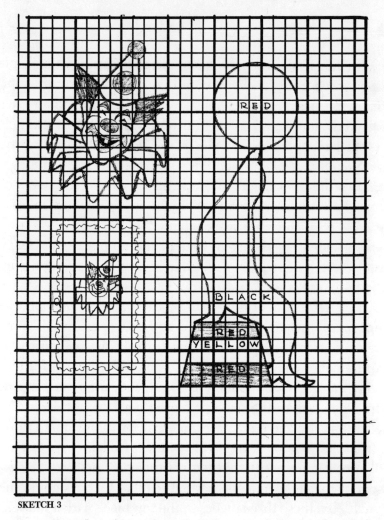

SKETCH 3

A very effective way to decorate the party area is the streamer
tent, using crepe-paper streamers with a centerpiece of balloons.
Start by placing a cup hook in the center of the ceiling area you are
using for your party. Wind one end of an 8-inch length of spool
wire around the hook; the remaining 6 inches will hold the ends of
the streamer tent. Cut four 36-inch lengths of string, and fasten the
ends to the spool wire that is fastened to the cup hook. Cut three

1-inch-wide strips from the long side of a 22- by 28-inch piece of tagboard (your art teacher can tell you where to get it). Join these strips with masking tape. You now have a circle about 84 inches wide. Make four small holes — one every 20 inches — and tie one of the four strings into each. This is the framework for the streamer tent (Sketch 4A). Cut 4-inch-wide streamers at least 46 inches long from two different colors of crepe paper, fifteen streamers of each color. Gather one end of these together, alternating colors. Wrap the ends with the wire attached to the cup hook. Then arrange them as shown in 4B, using four of the crepe-paper streamers to disguise the four strings of the framework. Now hang a cluster of balloons in the center.

Your refreshment table can be decorated in tiers of scalloped crepe paper, as in 4C. Cut, from the two colors of your color scheme, four strips in one color and two in the second color, each strip 14 inches wide and as long as your table. Repeat for the sides, cutting the strips only as long as the side. Scallop one edge of each strip. Do not make the scallops more than 2 inches deep. To make the scallop, use the edge of a large pan or dinner plate to trace as your model. Use one strip (full width) of each color to cover the tabletop, joining with a hidden seam (see *Basic Skills, Skill 3*). To assemble the cloth, join one tier to the other by taping it to the back of each. Join these three pieces to the top piece with a hidden seam. Repeat for the sides.

For the centerpiece, construct a Jack Horner Pie box with a clown's head made from a balloon (see 4D). Paint a clown's face on a white or pink inflated balloon. Give him a red nose, black eyes, dark eyebrows, and a red mouth. Glue his hair, red knitting wool cut in lengths of about 4 or 5 inches, to his head. You can give him a real clown's "frizz" if, after the glue dries, you fray the strands of

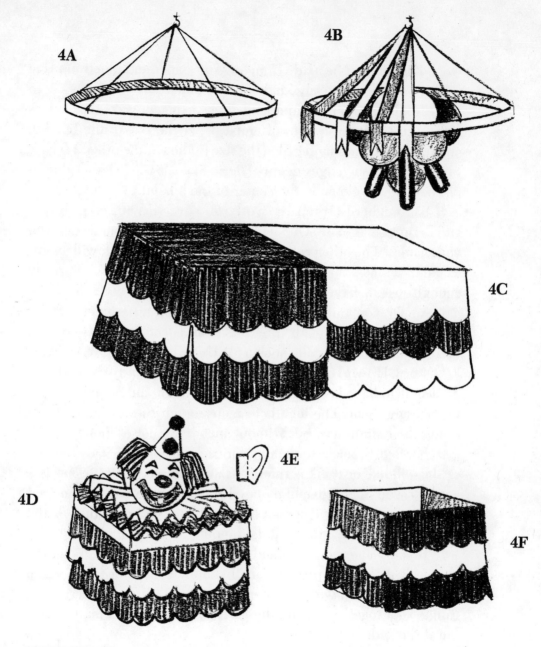

4A

4B

4C

4D

4E

4F

SKETCH 4

23

wool. His ears can be made from any stiff paper and glued in place (4E). For his hat, use any kind of small paper hat you find easy to make from construction paper and glue it in place. Make the clown's ruff by cutting two squares of crepe paper the size of the box lid, one square 2 inches larger than the size of the lid, the other 2 inches smaller. Flute the edges deeply (*Basic Skills, Skill 12*) and glue in place. Glue the clown in the center of the box lid.

You might also prepare two boxes covered with crepe paper and decorated as in 4F. One will hold all the things you need to run your games. The other will contain whatever prizes you will award to game winners. (You might not have prizes at all — it is really enough just to have the gaiety of the party and the fun of the games.) Or you might make gag crowns for all winners. Make simple paper crowns with "precious stones" crayoned in here and there, adding a gag saying such as WINNER AND NEW CHAMPION or CHAMPION CHICKEN PLUCKER, and so on. If you do decide to have favors and prizes, use humor and common sense in choosing them. The idea is to amuse your guests or give them things they might use, but without spending a lot of money.

For favors, select something for each person that you know he or she will like or think is funny. As an example, if one friend is a car buff, you might give him one of the matchbox toy cars, priced under one dollar. Or if money is a problem, find a picture of the kind of car he likes, cut it out, and mount it on a piece of paper.

If you plan on favors, candy cups, funny hats, and so on, it is an excellent idea to provide small shopping bags or plain white lunch bags marked with each person's name. Then each guest's loot can be kept together during the party, thus avoiding a mad scramble at the end.

Circus Party Menu

Tomato Juice
Chicken Salad on Frank Roll
Ice Cream Cup   Ginger Ale

OR

Apple Juice
Cheese and Chili Burgers
Ice Cream Cones   Coke

OR

Refreshments for Afternoon Party

Make Your Own Sundae
(Assorted ice creams, assorted toppings, nuts, and sprinkles)

Ice Cream Cup

6 ounces semisweet chocolate
  bits
2 tablespoons butter

1 pint ice cream
¼ cup crushed peppermint
  candy

Melt chocolate and butter over hot water. Line muffin pan with 6 fluted paper baking cups and coat cups with chocolate mixture. Chill for at least 1 hour. Peel away paper, leaving chocolate cups. Fill with ice cream and sprinkle with peppermint candy. Serves 6.

Cheese and Chili Burgers

3 pounds ground beef
1 teaspoon salt
Freshly ground black pepper
Butter

12 hamburger buns
Onion rings
Cheese Sauce or chili sauce

Combine ground beef, salt and pepper. Mix well. Divide into 12 hamburgers and broil. Butter rolls. Serve burger on bun with onion ring and a choice of Cheese Sauce or chili sauce. Serves 12.

Cheese Sauce

½ pound Cheddar cheese,
  grated
1 cup milk

1 teaspoon dry mustard
½ teaspoon basil

Combine cheese, milk, mustard, and basil in top of double boiler. Cook over boiling water 15 minutes or until smooth, stirring frequently. Serve hot. (If it gets too thick, add a few tablespoons milk.)

Halloween Party

A Hallooween Party is always fairly traditional. Your decorations will be about the same as for all Halloween parties — ghosts, black cats, witches, grinning pumpkins, and a skeleton or two. The general idea is to be as colorful as possible and yet sort of spooky.

Supplies

balloons
construction paper
crepe paper, orange and black
hatbox or box of similar size
starch, liquid, and also spray starch if you are hanging decorations
paintbrushes
poster paints, black and orange, if you are making decorations
ribbon
string
tape
wrapping paper, brown and white, in rolls if possible

Remember: all leftover supplies should be kept in your party box. You'll find that they come in handy.

Let's start with the front door. There are lots of choices, but this time simple and easy will be the password. You can use either the witch-broom-moon combination or the owl, cat, or pumpkin heads as shown in Sketch 5. (Halloween Party sketches are on pages 28, 29, and 31.)

The inside decorations can be drawings of all sizes on wrapping paper, or you can obtain die-cut forms of the above mentioned characters from most variety stores. Place them around the party area to give a general feeling of gay spookiness. You can do this by taping them to your wall with clear tape — not, however, if you have wallpaper! If your walls are papered, make your decorations from crepe paper or colored construction paper, stiffen them with spray starch and a warm iron, and hang them on strings taped to the ceiling.

You can usually find a skeleton, packaged and ready to scare,

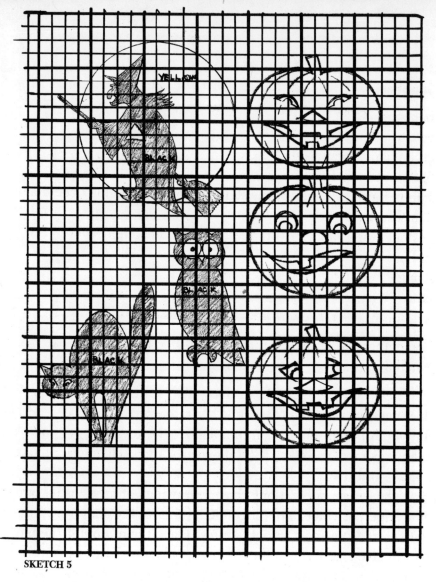

SKETCH 5

at a store during this holiday season. If you are a great "maker," see Sketch 6 for ideas. (All these figures can be scaled as in *Basic Skills, Skill 4* to whatever size you want and placed around the party area.)

Your table for plates, napkins, cups, utensils, and various

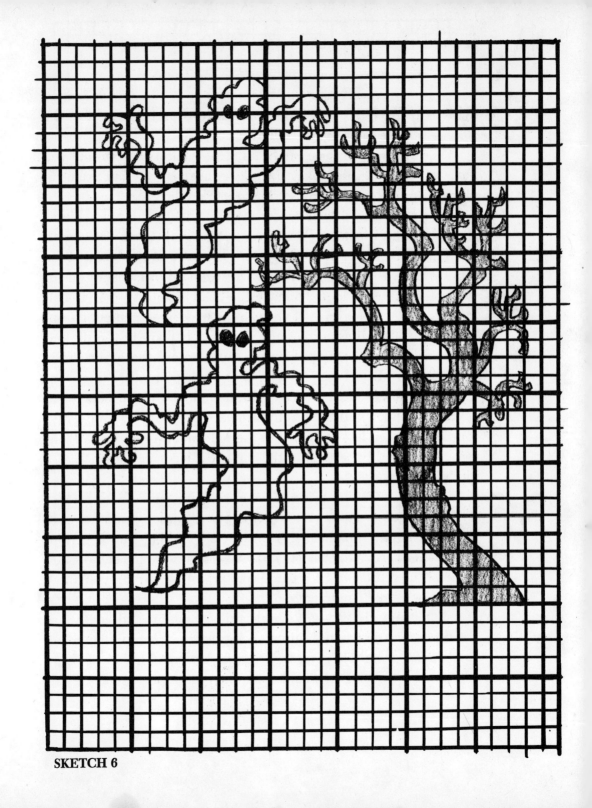

SKETCH 6

goodies can have a cloth made of crepe paper, as in Sketch 7. Such items as paper plates, cups, and napkins can all be bought at the store — you see them every Halloween.

The table centerpiece can be an actual jack-o'-lantern that you have carved from a pumpkin. Face styles are suggested in Sketch 5, or you can make one of those shown in Sketch 7.

Use the same directions for making the Jack Horner Pie as shown for the Birthday Party (page 18) — with these exceptions. Use orange crepe paper to cover both the sides of the box and the top. Decorate the paper with either a cardboard black cat or one of the jack-o'-lantern faces. To make the head, inflate an orange balloon and paint a face on it. If you want to make a permanent pumpkin head, follow these directions. Inflate a balloon to the desired size. Cut 1½-inch strips of crepe paper across the grain (*Basic Skills, Skill* 5). Dip these into a bowl of liquid starch, wetting completely. Squeeze out the excess starch from the crepe paper and cover the balloon with at least three layers. Allow to dry for twenty-four hours. Then let the air out of the balloon and remove it. Paint the dried crepe paper, using the pumpkin faces in Sketch 5 as a guide.

Again, favors and prizes depend on your pocketbook and/or your imagination. Perhaps it is best to play it for laughs rather than to spend money. For favors, have pieces of ribbon running from your centerpiece. Attach a gag gift for each guest to the end of each ribbon. The gift could be a cutout picture of something you know each guest would like to have.

For game prizes, such simple things as gum and candy are always good. You could disguise each prize in wrapping paper — a single piece of bubble gum, for example, wrapped in lots of tissue and finished off with an outside wrapping of crepe paper.

SKETCH 7

Halloween Party Menu

Tomato Juice
Creamed Chicken in Pastry Shells
Raw Carrots and Celery
Frozen Pops

31

OR

Vegetable Soup
Seeded Roll Sandwiches
Coleslaw   Pickles
Pumpkin Pie

OR

Refreshments for Afternoon Party

Orange Ice   Brownies
Cold Drinks

Frozen Pops

Mix ½ cup orange-flavored instant breakfast drink powder with ¼ cup sugar and 2 cups warm water. Freeze in small paper cups until nearly solid. Stick in plastic spoon or fork for handles. When completely frozen, tear off paper cups. Makes 8 pops.

Seeded Roll Sandwiches

Have available ham, salami, bologna, cheese, and so on, and rolls, as well as lettuce, mayonnaise, and mustard. Let your guests do their own thing.

Monster Party

This is another occasion you can play for laughs. In planning this party, first try to create a sense of far-out fun. Your invitation problems will be a bit different. To be sure, you must include the where-and-when information, but this time everyone must bring his own box mask. Since not all your guests will know how to make box masks, you must enclose a few basic suggestions with your invitations or arrange to have your guests take a look at this book. (Monster Party sketches are on pages 34, 36, 38, and 40.)

Supplies

balloons, round and long (for monster heads and noses)
brush, about ¼ inch (for very large areas, you'll want a larger brush)
cardboard boxes in various sizes for monster-making
crepe paper, black, yellow, and green
Dixie cups
knitting yarn
masking tape
paper bags
pipe cleaners
poster board or white cardboard
poster paints: red; mix red and black for brown
                black; mix black and yellow for green
                yellow; mix yellow and red for orange
spool wire
tissue paper
transparent tape
wire hangers
wrapping paper, brown

Box masks are not hard to make (see Sketches 8 and 9). Mask 8A is a cardboard box, about 12 to 14 inches wide, 24 inches long, and about 12 inches deep. Cut out a place on each side (see dotted lines) for your shoulders. Make monster hair by using 5-inch-wide strips of any color crepe paper, cutting them in lengths to match the length of your box. Fringe all but the last inch as in 8B (see *Basic*

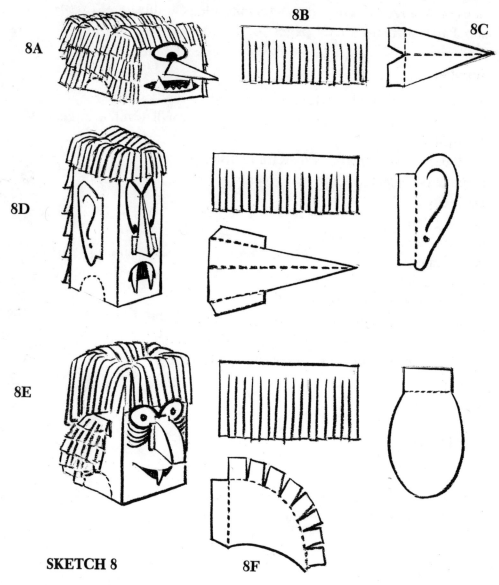

8A

8B

8C

8D

8E

SKETCH 8

8F

Skills, Skill 8). Put the hair on by taping the uncut straight edge to the box. Start with the lowest layer, overlapping the next layers enough to hide the tape. For the top, tape the straight edge to the front edge of the "head"; flap the fringe over. For the nose, use cardboard or several thicknesses of wrapping paper glued together. Cut a shape, as in 8C, fold along the dotted lines, and tape to the box. The eye and mouth should be painted black, but not until you have painted the non-hairy part of the box whatever color monster you wish to be.

Masks 8D and 8E are made the same way. The nose for mask 8E is a little more difficult. Cut two pieces, as in 8F. Fold along the dotted lines, first cutting up to the dotted line all the lines indicated by the double line — along the bridge of the nose on both pieces. When you tape the two pieces together on the inside of the bridge, the curve of the nose will be maintained.

Be sure to cut eye holes in all masks.

Sketch 9 shows ideas for masks made with brown paper bags. Get a bag large enough to go over your head with comfort, and have an extra bag or two on hand in case you tear one.

Mask 9A is the easiest to make. The hair is the same as for mask 8A. The eyes, nose, and mouth are painted with poster paint, using black and some lighter color for the hooded eyes. Make the tooth white. If the bag is fairly deep, put some crushed tissue paper or newspaper inside the top to keep the bag in shape.

Mask 9B consists mostly of painting the face. But for the nose use a salami-shaped balloon fastened to the bag with transparent tape. For the hair, cut any color tissue into 1-inch squares. Hold each square flat by one corner, then place a pencil with an eraser on the end firmly in the middle of the square. Turn the pencil clockwise. This twists the paper into points. Cover the area of the bag

9A

9B

9C

9D

9E

SKETCH 9

36

that is to have hair with glue and while still wet, cover with the twisted tissue.

Mask 9C is made with two bags to give the high-rise head look. The eyes are painted on; the nose is a partially inflated balloon taped to the bag. The teeth (9D) are cut from cardboard or stiff white paper. Fold along the dotted line and cut the short double line up to the dotted line. Slit the bag along the upper lip, which you have made with a brush and poster paint. Insert the shaded part through the slit and tape it on the inside of the bag. Stuff the second bag half full of newspaper — if you want a really tall head, stuff it up to the last 2 inches. Slip this bag over the other and tape. Make the hair as in mask 8A. Remember, the hair strips should be much wider than 5 inches unless you want lots of layers of short hair.

Mask 9E calls for painted eyebrows, mouth, and teeth. The nose is a Dixie cup taped in place and painted. The eyes are two white balloons, partially inflated, with a black dot painted in the center of each. Tape them in place with transparent tape. The hair is the same as for 8A.

Tell your guests to arrive with their masks on. As they come in, pin a large number on each guest, and give him or her a slip of paper and a pencil. After all the guests have arrived, tell them to write down which person belongs to which number. (This means that everyone should know everyone else and should, therefore, disguise their voices to fool each person they talk to.) When all the lists are complete, have the unveiling. Get some simple prizes (maybe oversized lollypops) for those who guessed the most correct identities.

For your general decorations, you might keep the expenses down by using a few signs, 10 inches long and 8 inches deep, as in

MONSTER RALLY TODAY Bring your own HEAD	HAVE A MONSTER GOOD TIME!
TODAY IS MONSTER DAY!	ALL MONSTERS PLEASE LEAVE EXTRA TEETH HERE ↓
GOOD MONSTERS DON'T LEAVE BONES AROUND	BAD MONSTERS TURN INTO PEOPLE... BEWARE!
PAGING DR. FRANKENSTEIN	MONSTER IS BEAUTIFUL!

SKETCH 10

Sketch 10. Wherever you put a sign, make a box monster to stand there as though he is holding it.

The box monsters are all made with boxes and/or balloons, crepe paper, heavy wrapping paper, and wire hangers (Sketch 11).

The Single-tooth Fingeldank (11A) is a rectangular grocery box. Cut along the dotted line for the legs. The head is a round balloon with a long balloon for a nose. The hair is made of short pieces of knitting yarn glued to the balloon. The eyes, mouth, and tooth are painted on with poster paints. The arms are cut from heavy wrapping paper, as are the feet. Fold at the dotted line on each end and attach with transparent tape.

The Mini-haired Waffelfink (11B) is mostly round balloons. Inflate one as large as possible, the second a bit smaller for the head, and a long one for the nose. Tape together. Paint in the eyes and mouth with black poster paint. Cut out the ears and teeth from white paper (11C) and glue into place. Cut the feet from heavy wrapping paper and glue to the bottom of the body balloon. Link six pipe cleaners together in pairs (11D). When you have three strands double length, twist them together so the arms are sturdy. Leave the last 1 inch free for fingers. Cut a lot of short strands of knitting yarn. Spread glue on the area you want covered with hair and glue in place.

The Four-footed Oomsplat (11E) is the same kind of box as 11A. Cut as indicated by the dotted line on all three sides for its legs. The arms and feet are also the same as 11A. The eyes and mouth are painted on. The nose is cut from heavy white paper in the shape indicated (11F). Fold along the dotted line and tape into place. The crepe-paper hair is as explained for mask 8A.

The Square-headed Schlumph (11G) is a somewhat more square type of box. The eyes, mouth, and teeth are painted on. The

11A

11B

11C

11D

11E

11F

11H

11G

SKETCH 11

40

nose is a long-shaped balloon. The pattern for the horns is shown in 11H. The arms and feet are the same as for the other monsters.

Notice that each monster is holding a staff. This is made by taping two straightened wire hangers together, making a foot at one end as for the trunk of the balloon tree in the Balloon Party directions (page 13). Tape the monster signs to the staffs.

Use one of the ideas for construction of the refreshment table that are in the plans for the Western Frontier Days Party (page 60). For table decorations, use black crepe paper for the tablecloth. Decorate the sides with cutout monster eyes and teeth as shown in sketch.

The table centerpiece can be a Jack Horner Pie box, Sketch 2, page 18. Place your own monster on the top.

Monster Party Menu

Tremendous Hero

Pickles	Potato Chips

Watermelon

Canned Soft Drinks

OR

Tuna Submarines

Carrot Sticks	Tiny Tomatoes
Cupcakes	Soft Drinks

OR

Refreshments for Afternoon Party

Chocolate Cake   Lemonade   Ice Cream Dixie Cups   Nuts

Tremendous Hero

Italian bread, around 3 feet long. Fill with layers of ham, salami, cheese, tomato, lettuce, mustard, sliced pickle, and so on. Can be cut into individual portions — causes lots of comment and couldn't taste better. Serves 12 or more.

Tuna Submarines

¾ cup mayonnaise
2 tablespoons lemon juice
1 teaspoon milk
½ teaspoon granulated sugar
½ teaspoon salt
¼ teaspoon dillweed

7-ounce can tuna, drained
3 tablespoons chili sauce
1 long loaf Italian bread, split
Lettuce
2 cups shredded cabbage

About 20 minutes before serving, in medium bowl make dressing: stir ½ cup mayonnaise, 1 tablespoon lemon juice, milk, sugar, salt, and dillweed. In small bowl with fork, flake tuna, stir in ¼ cup mayonnaise, chili sauce, and 1 tablespoon lemon juice. Thinly spread bread with mayonnaise. On bottom half, arrange lettuce, top with tuna mixture. Toss cabbage with dressing and arrange on tuna. Top with remaining bread. Slice crosswise into sandwiches. Serves 6.

Project Parties

A good way to have fun and also to help someone else at the same time is a project party. For example, the children in the wards of any hospital always need some special little attentions, and rarely get enough. This is a party to make things for them.

First, call your local hospital and tell them what you want to do. Ask for details about how many children there are, how old they are, how many boys, and how many girls. Perhaps your family doctor can be helpful in putting you in touch with the right person in the hospital volunteer office.

Children who are not old enough to read are the hardest to keep entertained. For this age group, plan on making toy trains and cuddly stuffed animals at your Project Party. Invite both boys and girls, if possible, and divide the jobs.

Aside from refreshments, this type of party is spent making something, so you won't need any decorations. Save your money, skill, and energy for the toys.

Supplies

Milk Carton Train:

brass paper fasteners
brush
cans, 10-ounce, one for each engine
caps from small bottles
construction paper, yellow
felt marking pen (this will make a mark on waxed cartons)
milk cartons, at least 8 for each train
plastic straws
plastic wood
poster paints, black, red, and yellow
spools, 1 for each train
twine, medium weight

Stuffed Toys:

calico (or other material), ⅓ yard for each cat
checked gingham (or other material), ⅓ yard for each dog
cotton, 1 large package for each animal
felt, pink, black, green, and red
needles and thread
ribbon, ½ yard for each animal

For the toy trains, ask your guests to save milk cartons for at least a week before the party. (Project Party sketches are on pages 46, 47, and 49.)

Milk Carton Train: In making any cuts in the cartons, you should first make an entrance slit with a sharp knife.

The first carton is to be cut as shown in Sketch 12A. Cut along the dotted lines. You will need a Magic Marker or a felt marking pen to make a mark on the heavily waxed cartons. The top of the carton is used as a cowcatcher for the front of the engine. Flip A over, put glue on the sides and front, and put A inside of 12B.

Take another carton and cut along the dotted lines as in 12C. Glue carton C into place as in 12D.

For the barrel of the engine, use a 10-ounce soup can, remove the label, and glue into B as shown in 12D.

Cut the wheels from a third carton. Use jar or bottle tops in two different sizes as patterns. (Or use *Basic Skills, Skill 2* to make two patterns from cardboard.) The 10-ounce can is a perfect pattern for the large wheel, while the small front wheel can have a pattern with a diameter of 2 inches. You should be able to get six large and six small wheels from one carton (12E). With a nail or the end of your scissors, make a hole in the center of each wheel, and also ones on the engine body where the wheels are to be mounted.

Glue together three wheels of each size. Cut ⅛-inch washers from a plastic straw. Put a brass paper fastener through the hole in each wheel, add the washer, and then put it into the proper place on the engine.

The smokestack is a wooden spool, and the headlight is a screw-top bottle cap. Plastic wood will be needed to mount them. Have someone hold the wooden spool in place while you fill in around the bottom of it. When this little "platform" is finished, allow it to dry. If the platform is not sticking to the engine, glue it in its proper place and then glue the spool to the platform. For the headlight, fill the screw-top cap with plastic wood. When the plastic wood is dry you can glue it to the front of the engine. To give the effect of a light, cut a piece of yellow construction paper the size of the cap and glue it on.

For the coal car, see Sketch 13. Unfold the peaked part (13A) of the milk carton. The carton should look like 13B. Cut along the dotted lines (13B), fold inward, and tape. The carton should be square.

Sketch 13C shows where to cut for the body shape. When cut, it should look like the non-shaded area. Fold up the end 2¼ inches and glue into place. Using what you can of the rest of the carton and another whole one, cut twelve wheels the size of the front wheel of the engine.

The freight car is very easy. Use the instructions from the coal car to square off the carton, then cut four holes in what will be the bottom of the car (13D). The holes should be large enough to allow a finger to get in to bend the brass paper fasteners to mount the wheels. Cut two more holes, one in each end of the car, so you can couple the car to another car. Paint the freight car yellow or red.

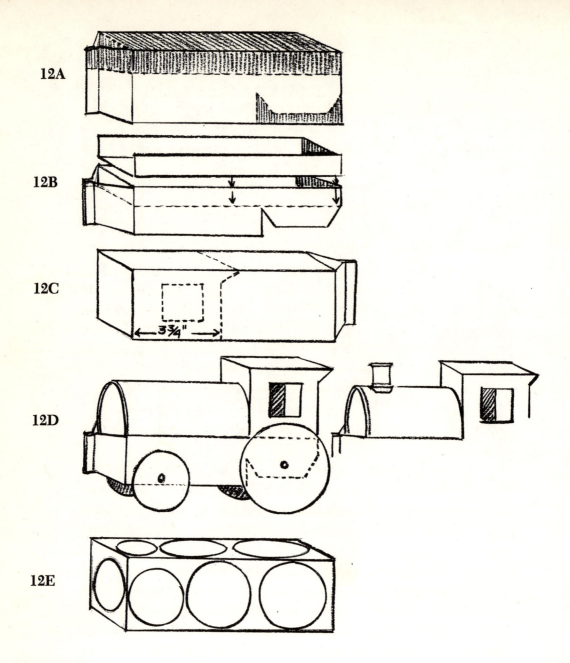

12A

12B

12C

3¾"

12D

12E

SKETCH 12

46

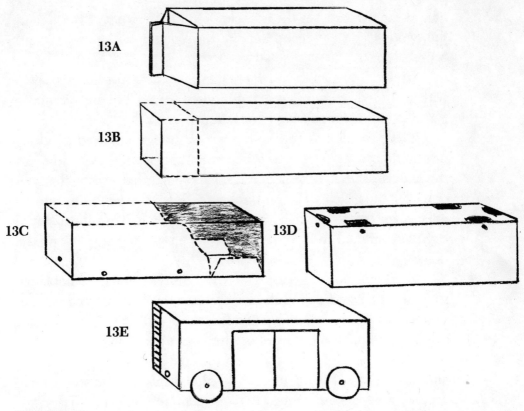

13A

13B

13C

13D

13E

SKETCH 13

When dry, use a small brush to outline the doors and end ladders (13E). Cut the wheels as for the engine and coal car. Make as many freight cars as you want, varying the colors. The engine and coal car should be black to contrast with the freight cars.

Each train car can be attached to another with twine. Take a piece of twine about 4 inches long, long enough to put a knot in each end with a little space between. Knot one end of the twine. Starting with the engine, thread the unknotted end of the twine through the hole in the rear end of the engine and then through the hole at the front end of the coal car. Tie another knot at this end of the twine. Continue "coupling" in this manner to the end of your train.

Stuffed Toys: Every small child loves to carry around and sleep with a stuffed animal that is soft and cuddly. Here are directions (see Sketch 14) for making two stuffed animals.

Trace the dog sketch on the wrong side of checked gingham or other material, leaving a ½-inch margin beyond the outline of the pattern. This is necessary when making stuffed toys so that you don't put too much strain on the seams. Sew all around, leaving an open space through which you insert the stuffing. Turn the material right side out and stuff. When the dog is plump enough, sew up the hole.

The pattern for the ears is shown. This time you need not leave so wide a margin beyond the seam, as the ears will not be stuffed. Stitch the ears inside out, leaving the top open. Turn the ears right side out and tack to the head on the bias, as shown.

Make the eyes, eyebrows, and nose of black felt, the mouth and tongue of red felt. Cut out and glue in place. After the glue is dry, use a needle and thread to make completely secure. Tie a ribbon around the neck.

Cut out the cat pattern (from calico or other material) and proceed exactly as you did with the dog — except for the ears. These ears are part of the main pattern. Sew them inside out as you do the rest of the pattern until you turn the material. Then tack the ears closed with needle and thread.

Cut the large part of the eyes from green felt, the pupils and nose from black felt. The mouth and tongue are pink felt. Glue in place, and when dry, tack with a needle and thread. Give the cat a ribbon collar, too.

SKETCH 14

Project Party Menu

Spaghetti
Italian Bread   Mixed Green Salad
Lime Sherbet   Cookies
Hawaiian Punch

OR

Baked Ham   Macaroni and Cheese
Rolls   Mixed Green Salad
Fruit   Cookies
Ginger Ale

Because there is so much to do, perhaps your guests could arrive right after lunch, work until 6:00 P.M., and then stop for dinner.

Spaghetti Sauce

3 tablespoons vegetable oil	Salt and pepper
1 pound chopped beef	¾ teaspoon oregano
2 medium-sized onions, diced	2 small cans tomato paste
4 tablespoons chopped parsley	2 large cans Italian tomatoes
1 clove garlic, crushed	Parmesan cheese

Heat oil in large Dutch oven. Add meat and brown. Add onions, parsley, garlic, salt, pepper, and oregano. Stir over medium heat until onions are soft. Add tomato paste. Stir in well before adding Italian tomatoes. Stir and break up whole tomatoes. Bring to a boil, reduce heat, cover and let simmer for 2 hours, stirring occasionally. Serve over thin spaghetti cooked according to package directions. Sprinkle with Parmesan cheese.

Valentine Party

This party theme may be a favorite with girls. The idea is to make your party especially pretty.

Supplies

Bristol board or cardboard, 4 or 5 sheets, white
crepe paper, pink, white, red
hatbox or box of similar size
lace paper doilies
tape — masking, double-stick, and transparent
spool wire

The outside doorway can be treated as in Sketch 15A. (Valentine Party sketches are on pages 52 and 53.) The cupid (15B) and the heart (15C) can be made in any size by following the number square formula (see *Basic Skills, Skill 4*).

The door decoration (15A) needs lace paper doilies, white Bristol board or cardboard, and red and pink crepe paper. Cut out the main heart, its size being governed by your front door panel. Use 15C for cutting all hearts, no matter what size. Surround the heart with lace doilies, and cut three streamers of red crepe paper to hold the hanging hearts. Tape these streamers to the back of the heart and then attach the smaller pink hearts. Draw your cupid (15B) on the Bristol or white cardboard, remembering to draw your scaling squares in lightly so that they can be erased. Paint the cupid pink and place in the center of the heart.

For the interior party area, use much the same directions as for the Circus Party with the streamer tent. Alternate crepe-paper

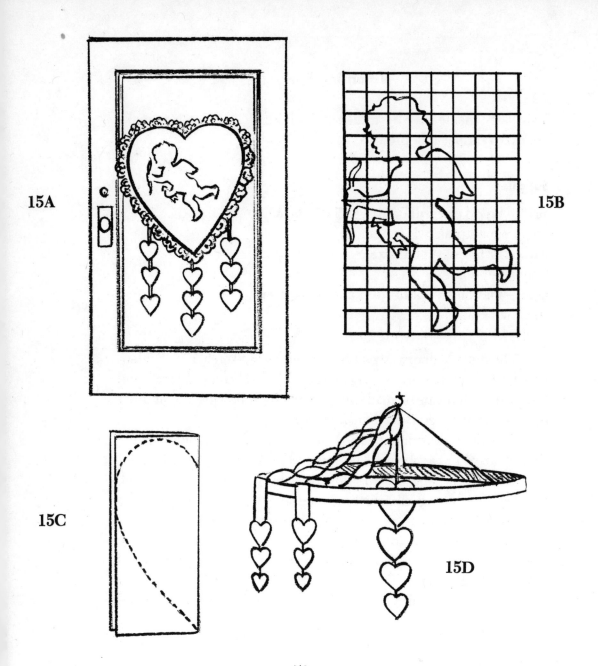

15A

15B

15C

15D

52

SKETCH 15

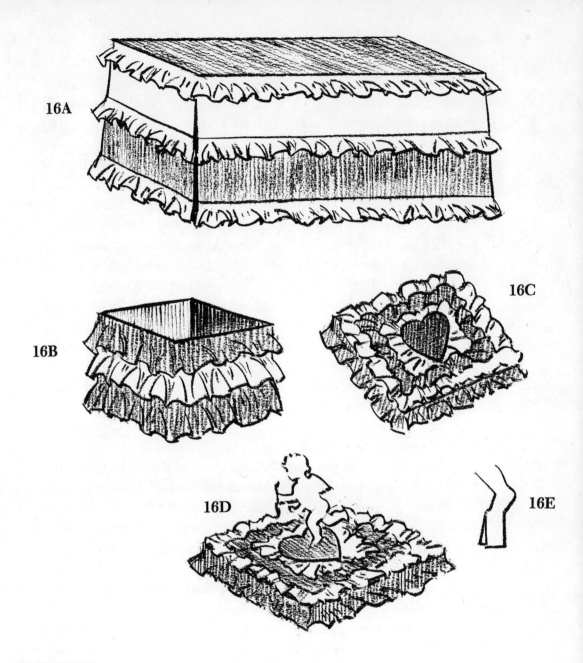

16A

16B

16C

16D

16E

SKETCH 16

53

streamers of white, red, and pink, twisting each streamer half a dozen times before hanging it, and suspending hearts from each streamer. In the center hanging down will be a teardrop of hearts, graduated in size (15D).

Sketch 16A shows a pink and white crepe-paper cloth for the party table. Most tables are 36 inches wide, so you would cut your paper into 18-inch widths. (To join, see *Basic Skills, Skill 3*.) The top will require four panels, two for the actual top, and one each for the back and the front. Use pink crepe paper for these panels. The length of each panel will be determined by the length of the table with enough left over to provide the first tier on each side. Use white crepe paper for the last tier. As tables are usually 30 inches from the floor, each tier should be 15 inches deep. The tabletop edge and the edge of each tier are trimmed with strips of crepe paper 6 inches wide, either deeply fluted *(Basic Skills, Skill 12)* or trimmed all the way around with lace doilies cut in half and taped in place. Be sure to leave each corner slit from the floor to the table-top. This lessens the chance of tearing the cloth or pulling it off the table if someone should accidentally bump into it.

The table centerpiece can be a variation of the Jack Horner Pie used for other parties. Divide the height of the Jack Horner Pie box into three equal measurements. Cut your contrasting strips of crepe paper the same size (16B). Flute the edges and tape into place starting at the bottom and overlaying each strip enough to hide the top of the strip below. Cover the top (16C) with a fluted strip for the edge. Then cut three squares, each square 1 inch or 1½ inches smaller than the other. Flute the edges. Tape together, and then tape the assembled pieces to the top of the box. Cut a heart from Bristol board or cardboard and place it in the center of the box top. Now cut a cupid (16D) from Bristol board or cardboard, scaling it up to about 6 inches high (*Basic Skills, Skill 4*). Extend the lower foot with a tab about 2 inches long (16E). Put another piece the same size next to it. Now slit the center of the top of the box, slip the two tabs through, and bend back on the tape. Cupid should be painted pink before it is put in place.

Valentine Party Menu

Cream of Tomato Soup
Chicken Salad Sandwiches (heart-shaped, of course)
Sliced Cranberry Jelly   Flowered Radishes
Pink Frosted Cupcakes with Cinnamon Candy Center

OR

Chicken Soup
Peanut Butter and Jelly Sandwiches (heart-shaped, of course)
Strawberry Ice Cream   Pink Lemonade

OR

Refreshments for Afternoon Party

Heart-shaped Layer Cake   Apples-on-a-Stick
Pink Lemonade

Heart-shaped Layer Cake

Any cake with white frosting, outlined with tiny cinnamon hearts.

Apples-on-a-Stick

One perfect apple for each guest. If appropriate sticks are not obtainable, use plastic picnic forks for handles. Dip into glaze made as follows:

2 cups sugar   ¼ teaspoon cream of tartar
1 cup water   Red food coloring

Combine first 3 ingredients and stir over low heat until sugar dissolves. Boil without stirring until syrup begins to darken (310° F.). Remove from heat and place in larger pan of cold water to stop boiling instantly. Stir in few drops of red food coloring. Remove from cold water and place in larger pan of hot water during dipping. Place apples on well-greased surface to harden. (Covers 8 large apples.)

Western Frontier Days Party

Time for fun western style! This party is planned for outdoor entertaining — you might even have the party in a local park — but you can also rearrange the ideas very successfully indoors.

Supplies

brush, ¼ inch
cardboard for signs, 2 or 3 sheets, white
crepe paper, various colors
poster paint, black
tape
twine, medium weight
wrapping paper, brown

To welcome your guests, use either or both the cowboy on the bucking bronco and the sign as shown in Sketch 17. (Western Frontier Days Party sketches are on pages 57, 59, 60, and 61.) If the bronco seems a bit complicated, use just the sign and color it in light brown paint. If your friends are coming dressed in cowboy or Indian costumes, place some signs just inside the gateway:

PARK YOUR GUNS AND BOW AND ARROW HERE.
NO FIGHTING BEYOND THIS POINT.
PLEASE MUFFLE YOUR SPURS.
TODAY IS INDIAN LADIES DAY.

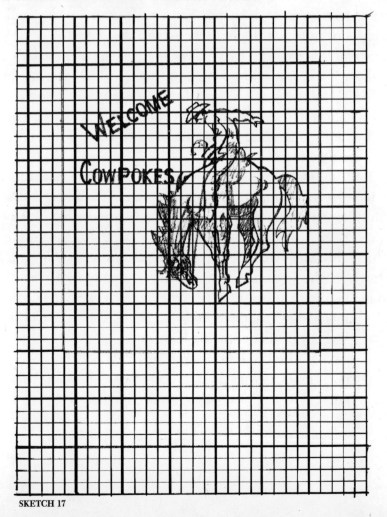

SKETCH 17

Outdoor decorations will, of course, be less elaborate than those indoors. Sketch 18 shows two suggestions for indoor decorations.

The crepe-paper "murals" look harder than they really are. Sketch 18A simply involves cutting strips from five different colors of crepe paper. This panel could cover one wall behind the refreshment table. Numbers 1 and 3 are light grass green, 2 is light blue for the river, 4 a dark green for the distant hills, 5 a darker blue for the mountains, and 6 yellow for the sun. (Scale this up by using *Skill 4* in *Basic Skills*, except that each 1-inch square shown should equal 2 feet.) Cut each shape. Tape each shape to the wall with double-stick tape, overlapping the edges.

Scene 18B could be treated as a night scene in a western town. Numbers 1 and 2 would be cut from either black or navy blue, 3 should be a light enough blue to show up against 1, 2, and 5. Number 4 is pale yellow, and 5 should be a blue that is lighter than 1, 2, and 3. Start by covering the wall area with color 5, then 3 and 4. Last, tape up 1 and 2.

Refreshments can be served in two areas. For your soft-drink bar, tape brown wrapping paper around an ironing board as shown in 19A. Keep a tub full of ice with your drinks resting in it behind the bar. With an eye on the clean-up job, try to buy all your drinks in cans. This way everyone can use the cans as cups. Cover a large carton from the supermarket with brown wrapping paper. Place it beside the bar for all empties. (Remember to recycle the cans later.)

The second refreshment area, the table, can be set up next to the bar. Use one of the following ideas:

1. Two or three card tables put together (19B).
2. Two chairs, two wooden grocery boxes, and a piece of plywood (19C). A piece of ¼-inch plywood 2 feet wide by 6

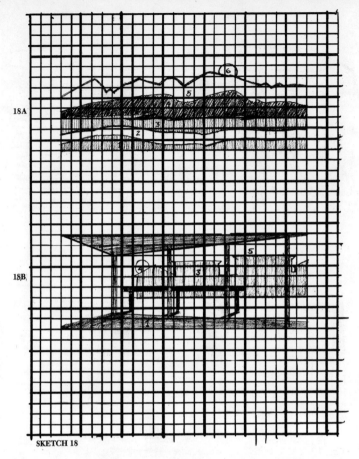

18A

18B

SKETCH 18

feet long can be obtained at a lumber yard for between $3.00 and 4.00. Or use the center leaves from your dining table.

Cover either of these with a red and white checkered paper tablecloth. If you can't find one, get a white one and paint red checks on it with poster paint. If you do paint the cloth, be sure the paint is not too thin because it will run. Test it on a paper napkin first.

Another idea for decorating the table is the chuck wagon. Use the same basic set up for the table — the painted wrapping paper would be the difference (19D).

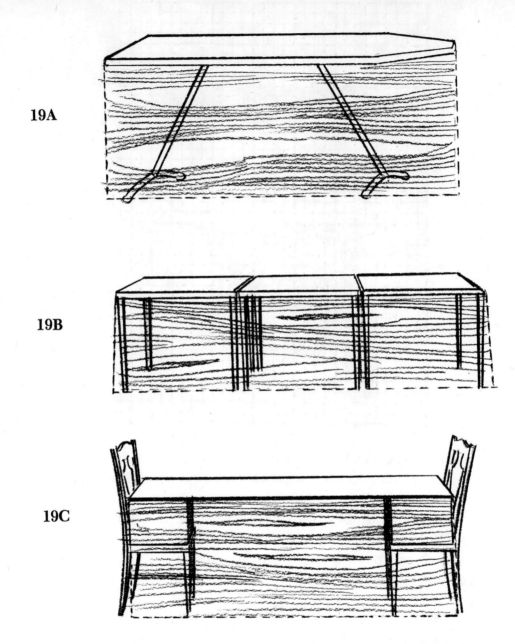

19A

19B

19C

SKETCH 19

19D

Western Party Menu

Baked Beans   Frankfurter and Roll
Coleslaw and Radishes
Gingerbread Cookies   Cider

OR

Sandwich Platter
Potato Chips   Pickles
Ice Cream Cake
Milk

OR

Refreshments for Afternoon Party

Orange Cup (Orange Sherbet topped wth Orange Slice)
Chocolate Chip Cookies   Soft Drinks

Sandwich Platter

Fill large plate with cream cheese and olives, lettuce and tomato, egg salad, plain peanut butter and peanut butter and jelly sandwiches. Let guests choose their own.

Orange Cup

Cut top third off orange, scoop out meat, scallop edges of shell. Fill with orange sherbet and decorate with orange slice.

Winter Party

A Winter Party theme is fun even if you live in an area where snow is unknown. The decorations are a joy to make and the general effect is great!

Supplies

cardboard or white paper
construction paper, black, orange, white, and another color, preferably bright
cotton
crepe paper, white and bright blue
double-stick tape
metallic foil
newspaper
thread, white cotton

Starting at the front door, make a non-melting snowman (Sketch 20). (Winter Party sketches are on pages 64, 65, and 66.)

First cover the inside panel of the door with bright blue crepe paper (see *Basic Skills, Skill 4*). Cut out the snowman's body and head from white paper or cardboard. His eyes, eyebrows, mouth, teeth, pipe, hat, and buttons are all made from black construction paper. Use a bright color for his scarf. Assemble as in 20A and tape to the blue center panel with double-stick tape. To make the snow, use small pieces of absorbent cotton held in place with glue.

The snowman's nose is made from orange construction paper (20B). Cut a shape as shown. Cut out the small V shapes so you can fold them back and make a base to be taped to the snowman's face with double-stick tape.

The inside decorations consist of lots of snowballs, snowflakes, and icicles. These should be hung all about the party area.

To make small snowballs, crush newspaper into a ball (20C). Cut 1-inch strips of white crepe paper and wind these around the crushed newspaper (20D) until you have a smooth snowball. Suspend from the ceiling with strong white cotton thread.

The icicles are 1-inch strips cut from silver metallic foil — curl the strips (20E) and pull them to the length you wish (20F). These can be suspended in clusters or as single icicles, using strong white cotton thread.

For snowflakes, see Sketch 21. Use 8- by 10-inch white construction paper. Fold in half, and fold that half in half. The dotted line shows the open edges. Trace these designs as in *Basic Skills, Skill 1*, and then cut away the shaded areas. These may be taped on the walls or suspended from the ceiling.

The table will have a blue paper tablecloth — or use blue crepe paper if you can't find a paper cloth the size you need. Tape some of the snowflakes you've made to the sides of the cloth with double-stick tape (Sketch 22A).

The table centerpiece will be a snowman again, sitting in the

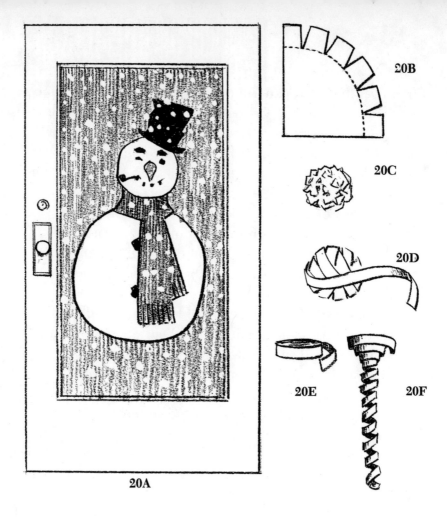

20B

20C

20D

20E   20F

20A

SKETCH 20

middle of an ice pond (22B). The pond is metallic foil cut in an irregular shape, surrounded by tufts of absorbent cotton patted down around the pond. Make a small snow island out of cotton and place it in the middle of the pond for the snowman. Make the body and head of the snowman as you did the snowballs. For the rest of him, follow the directions for making the front-door snowman.

SKETCH 21

22A

22B

SKETCH 22

Winter Party Menu

V-8 Juice
Fried Chicken
French Fries   Coleslaw
Rainbow Gelatin
Cookies   Milk

OR

Pizza Sandwiches
Raw Carrots, Celery, Radishes
Gingerbread   Cider

OR

Refreshments for Afternoon Party

Candies   Limed Grape Juice   Nuts
Coconut Cake

Rainbow Gelatin

Make lemon, strawberry, and lime gelatin according to package directions. Fill sherbet glasses with layers of each color.

Pizza Sandwiches

Small loaves French bread
Olive oil
Canned Italian tomatoes,
    drained and cut up
Grated Parmesan cheese

Sliced mozzarella cheese
Anchovy fillets
Canned meatballs, drained
Oregano and thyme

Cut loaves of bread in half lengthwise. Scoop out soft centers, leaving shells about ½ inch thick. Brush inside of shells with olive oil. Spread shells with tomatoes and sprinkle with Parmesan cheese. Put mozzarella and anchovies on some shells, mozzarella and sliced meatballs on others. Sprinkle with oregano, thyme, and oil. Bake at 400° F. for 15 minutes.

Limed Grape Juice

4 cups grape juice   2 tablespoons lemon juice

1 tablespoon lime juice   Club soda or ginger ale

Combine juices. Fill glasses with ice and pour juice mixture into glasses until about two-thirds full. Add club soda or ginger ale. Serves 6.

5

Party Games

Games are the fuel you use to keep the party mood in high gear. So, naturally, the games you choose are very important to the success of your party.

There are two good things to keep in mind when choosing your games. First, as nearly as possible, select those games you think will be fun for everyone, not just a few. And second, aim for a change of pace; don't choose all action games. One action game after another would make the pace too fast — and variety always helps to keep a party from becoming too boisterous.

If you want to, you can provide prizes for the winners of the games.

The following games are divided into three groups — active or outdoor games, games to begin or end a party, and quiet-time games.

Active Games

Balloon-blowing Race: Give every player a balloon, each one a different color, or tape the players' names on the balloons. Mark off a goal line as far away as your area permits. The players, on hands and knees, must blow their balloons over the goal. Remember, using hands is not allowed!

Balloon Boxing: Make a circle of twine large enough for two play-

ers to move about in. Arm the players with a balloon in each hand. Blindfold them and have them box with each other.

Balloon Race: Choose teams and give each team a balloon. At the signal, each team leader places the balloon between his legs and starts to run to the goal line and back. Then he hands the balloon to the next in line. He cannot use his hands to hold the balloon in place. Each player must do the same. The winning team is the one that finishes first. If the balloon breaks, the player must go back to the starting line and begin again with a new balloon.

Balloon Ten-Kicks: This is great for picnics, or where you can go barefoot. Take two balloons and stuff one inside the other. Fill with water. Each team lines up facing the other. The referee drops the balloon between them. A team must kick the ball ten times in a row to score a goal. As each player kicks, he shouts, 1, 2, 3, and so on. After a goal, the referee has another "kick off." No hands can be used.

Balloon Volleyball: Stretch string between two upright objects. Choose teams, each with a different colored balloon. Team A tries to get its own balloon over the string and at the same time keep Team B's balloon from touching the ground on A's side. Each time the balloon touches the ground, the team who owns it gets a point. The winner is the first team to reach 20 points.

Box Relay Races: Get packing boxes large enough for a player to get into. (You may be able to join two boxes together to get one big enough.) Remove the top and bottom, leaving only the sides. Drive sticks into the ground to make a zigzag racecourse. Choose teams. Each team member must step into the box, hold it off the ground, and run the course to the end and back.

Call Ball: Throw a soft rubber ball (or a basketball or beach ball) into the air and call one of the player's names. Everybody but the named player runs away. The named player must catch the ball and then call "stop." The runners must stop where they are. The player with the ball tries to hit one of the runners. The runner is allowed to dodge the ball, but he must always keep one foot in place. The runner who is hit first starts the play again. If no one is hit, the same player becomes "it" again.

Card or Orange Race: Form two lines. The first player in line holds a card between the tip of his nose and his upper lip. Without moving his feet, he must turn and transfer the card to the next team member, who must receive it between his nose and upper lip. (When using an orange, the player holds it between his shoulder and chin. He must turn around to transfer the orange to the next player.)

Chain Tag: Mark off two safety areas. Someone is "it." The others line up behind one safety area. When "it" yells "red," everyone runs for the other safety spot. "It" tries to tag as many players as possible before they get to the safety area. All those tagged join hands and form a chain "It" yells red again, and those in the safety area must run to the other safety area while the chain tries to tag them, but only the player who is "it," at one end of the chain, and the player at the other end can actually tag anyone.

Dodge Ball: Choose two teams. One forms a large circle, the other scatters inside it. The circle team throws a volleyball, basketball, or soft type of ball at the team inside the circle. Each time a player is hit, he must leave the circle. When the last player inside is hit, the teams change places. (This can also be played for more laughs with a water-filled double balloon.)

Feeding the Baby: Divide the players into pairs. Use a spoon or an eyedropper and a glass of water or soda. Each player must feed his partner the entire glass, a spoonful or an eyedropper at a time. The pair finished first wins.

Fish Race: Choose two teams. Each player gets a straw and each team gets a paper fish. At the starting signal, the first player of each team must pick up the fish from the ground by inhaling through the straw. He must hold the fish in that position up to the goal line and back. If he drops the fish, he must go back and start all over again. The team that finishes first is the winner.

Heel Race: Each player must reach the goal line by running the whole race on his heels. Toes are not allowed to touch the floor.

Keep Away: Choose teams. Use a ball, beanbag, or balloon. Each team tries to keep the ball away from the other team, but no player can hold it longer than 5 seconds. If he does, the ball goes to the other team.

Mounted Ball: This is good for a large group. Use a fairly large rubber ball. Set up a baseball diamond. Each player has a partner. When the batter hits the ball (he can use his hand instead of a bat), he must ride piggyback on his partner to first base. The outfielders must also ride piggyback to get the ball. They get off their mounts to retrieve the ball, but they must remount to throw it. Otherwise, regular baseball rules apply.

Paper Planes: Make paper airplanes. Each player gets three flights. Mark the longest of the three. The longest flight of all is the winner.

Peanut Toothpick Race: Line everyone up. Give each player a peanut and a toothpick. A player must race to the goal line on all fours with the toothpick in his mouth, rolling the peanut over the course.

Potato Race: Choose teams and appoint a potato collector for each. The collector gets a basket. Line the teams up in single file, about an arm's length apart. Place a potato at the left foot of each player. At "go," the first player picks up his potato, turns without moving his feet, and gives the potato to the person behind him. No player may pick up his potato until he receives one from the player in front of him. The second player has two potatoes to give to the third player and so on. The last player has all the potatoes. The potato collector takes all the potatoes from the last player and puts them in the basket. The first team to do so wins.

Rugged Relay Race: Choose two teams. The first player must run to the goal and back using one of four different gaits. He tags the next player, who runs the same gait. The first team to have all players run all four gaits is the winner. The gaits are:

1. the crab: the runner must do the crab walk on hands and feet, back toward the ground, feet toward the starting line.
2. the elephant: standing upright, the player must run with legs and arms kept absolutely straight and rigid.
3. the frog jump: the runner squats, his hands between his knees. He takes froglike jumps, landing on hands first, and then feet.
4. Indian file: each runner puts one foot directly in front of the other and "runs" the course.

Slow-Motion Circle Race: This race goes to the slowest. Form a large circle. Face right. Everyone starts to run as slowly as possible. The runner who touches or runs into the runner ahead must drop out. The slowest runner is the winner.

Stoop Race: Each player must bend forward and grasp his ankles. The first to reach the goal line in this position is the winner.

Tin Can Race: Each player gets two empty tin cans. He must stand with one foot on one can while he bends and picks up the other can and moves it ahead. Then he steps on the second can while he picks up the first and moves that ahead. And so on to the goal.

To and Fro Race: Line up everyone and point out the racecourse. This is run like every other race, except that when you blow a whistle, or yell "reverse," everyone must run in the opposite direction.

By the end of the race, no one will know which way they're going!
Wheelbarrow Race: Divide the guests into pairs. One player gets down on all fours and his partner picks up his feet, making him into a wheelbarrow. The race must be run in this way.

Beginning or Ending Games

The following are excellent ways to help start a party and also to end it. Even with only a few guests, these games create a lot of party spirit.

Are You a Bridge? Place three strong straight-backed chairs side by side, far enough apart so that the player's head rests on the seat of one outside chair and only his heels touch the other outside chair. Have him arch his back while you remove the middle chair. The player has to stay put, arms folded, for 10 seconds. (This is not as easy as it sounds if you don't have pretty strong stomach muscles.)

Balance: Place a widemouthed quart bottle — a milk bottle, orange juice or tomato juice bottle — in the middle of the floor standing up. Put a medium-sized hardcover book, not over 5- by 7-inches, over the mouth of the bottle. Have a player sit on it with his legs straight out in front, his left heel atop his right foot. Then have him lift both feet, hold his balance, and write his name on a pad so that it can be read.

Handkerchief Spearing: Place two straight-backed chairs facing each other, with about a 15-inch space in-between. Lay a broomstick from seat to seat. Place a large handkerchief over each corner of each chair back — four in all. Give the player a cane (or long stick) to hold in one hand. He must balance himself, feet off the ground and legs crossed, on the broomstick. Then he must lift the cane off the floor and, one at a time, remove the handkerchiefs with the cane. He is allowed to use the cane for balance in-between spearings.

Match Tricks: When you have just a few guests around at the beginning (or perhaps at the end) of a party, try these match tricks.

- Arrange 12 matches in 3 squares as shown.

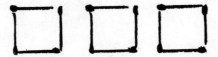

Ask a player to take away 2 matches and leave 2. The answer is shown below.

- Take 17 matches and make 2 rows of 3 squares each as shown.

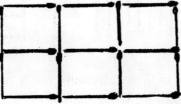

Ask a player to remove 5 matches and leave 3 squares. The answer is below.

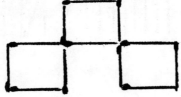

- Form 9 squares with 24 matches. Ask a player to remove 8 matches and leave 2 squares.

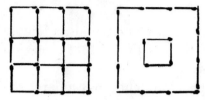

- Give a player 6 matches and ask him to form 3 and ½ dozen.

(3)   (6 = ½ dozen)

- Give a player 9 matches and ask him to make 10 — *without* breaking any.

- Make a row of 7 matches and ask a player to take away 1 and leave nothing.

(nil means nothing)

- Take 6 matches and ask a player to make 11 without breaking any.

(Roman numeral XI)

- For laughs, try these last two: Add 1 to 5 and make 4.

- Form a row of 6 matches. Add 5 more and make 9.

IIIIII NINE

Photograph: This is wonderful for the last 10 minutes of a party. Choose a victim. Then you, or someone who is a good talker and able to keep a straight face, take a camera without any film in it. Go about the room fussing with lights and really hamming it up. While you are pretending to get the right setting for the picture, blacken your fingers with burnt cork or pencil dust. Make a great point of getting the player's head in the right position, turning it this way and that, raising his chin — anything that will allow you to leave a smudge on his face without his suspecting it. Now snap the picture and ask if he would like to see a print. The answer is surely yes. Hand him a mirror.

Quiet Games

Art Game: Using old magazines or newspapers, cut out ears, noses, hair, eyes, cheeks, chins, and so on. Put each collection in a separate box — a box for noses, a box for ears, and so forth. Give each guest a blank piece of paper and tape. Tell him to choose a supply of needed parts from each box and make the craziest face he can with his selections. You can expand this game by supplying spare parts of the whole body.

Beat the Pan: Everyone is given some form of pan — a pie or cake tin, a small sauce pan — and a spoon of any size. One guest is asked to leave the room. While he is out, everyone decides what they want him to do when he comes back. The younger the guests, the more simple the task. By beating the pans, the players make the one who has been chosen do almost anything, from picking up a particular object to taking off John's left shoe and putting it on Mary's left foot. All the players beat their pans very slowly and softy when the "it" player starts out, louder and faster as he nears the designated object or person. If he starts to go away from the object, the group stops beating — then the "it" knows he has to go back where he was and continue until he has found the object. In the case of the shoe, once he has it in his hand continue beating so he will know that he has more to do with it, and so on until he finally gets it on Mary's foot. Absolutely no talking allowed!

Camouflage: A variation of treasure hunt. Select seven or eight everyday articles — a button, a fountain pen, a paper clip, a ring, a fork, and so on. Give everyone a paper and pencil and send them out of the room while you hide the objects. Example: put a dollar bill in among leaves of a plant, a paper clip on a piece of paper on a table, and so forth. Call everyone back in the room and tell them

78

how many and what objects you want them to look for. Nobody says a word. They just walk around and when they discover an object they write its location on the paper. The first to finish calls out "camouflage." This game can also be a good way to start a party. As each guest arrives, hand him a list and a pencil. Tell him to wander around and discover each item. He must not reveal the hiding spots to the others — just write them down on his list. The last guest to arrive will have to be given enough time for his search. Then see how many were "sleuth" enough to find them all.

Charades: Choose two teams. Each team member picks a famous book or song title or saying, being careful not to let the other team know what they have chosen. (The easiest names to use are sports figures, world leaders, and movie stars.) Each person on one team "acts out" one clue (no talking, no props) as to the identity of the charade. The opposing team gets one question only per team member. The team sits down after its charade has been guessed, the time it took is noted, and then the second team acts out its charade. The team guessing the correct identity in the shortest time wins.

Charity Drive Letter (or Fill in the Missing Words): This is great fun and lots of laughs for everyone! Form a circle. Take out the sheet of paper on which you have copied this letter. (It is easy to make up your own letter, too.) Ask each guest in turn for whatever kind of word is called for. Don't read the letter until the end. Just ask each person for whatever kind of word you need, such as the name of someone at the party, or an adjective, a number, or a celebrity. The result, when you read it aloud, will be something like this:

Dear **Betty**: _____
        name of one guest

    This is a plea for our well-known organization, the Society for

the Preservation of (**dirty   floors**). We are striving to reach a goal
                     adjective   noun
of (**2**) dollars to build a modern (**anteater**) for the less fortunate. We
   number   *noun*
know you, as one of the foremost (**chickens**) in your community,
                                  plural noun
will most certainly want to contribute (**milk**) to this (**stupid**) ven-
                                        noun   *adjective*
ture.

      Our president (**Mickey Mouse**) and our treasurer (**Joe Namath**)
              a movie star   *a sports figure*
have served with many (**rotten**) organizations. They beg you to dig
                      adjective
deep into your (**tulip beds**). Even if you can give only (**40 million**)
               plural noun   *number*
(**toenails**), it will make us (**cry**). The funds will allow us to obtain
nails   *verb*
an (**ice cream soda**) at least every (**20 years**).
   noun   *period of time*
    This will be a (**blue**) monument to your (**face**). People will
              adjective   *noun*
come and have our (**wheelbarrow**) take care of their (**mothers**) and
                  noun   *plural noun*
other things.

    We hope this will someday help stamp out (**convertibles**) com-
                                          plural noun
pletely.

Sincerely,

Signed: (**Dr. Frankenstein**)
        a celebrity

Crazy Story Game: Have your guests sit in a circle on the floor. As host or hostess, you start off with a sentence or two, such as "The boy rushed down the street yelling . . ." Then stop and point to someone in the circle to start at once to continue your sentence. Then he points to someone else, and so on. The less sense the story makes, the funnier it gets — particularly if you have imaginative friends.

Folded Portraits: Pass out sheets of paper and a pencil to each player. Everyone draws a head, either of a person or an animal, in the upper third of the paper. Fold the sheet so that only the neckline shows, and then pass it to the next player. He draws the arms and body of a person or the legs and body of an animal in the second third of the paper, folds it over to hide what has been drawn, and passes it on to the player next to him. Now the legs of either a person or an animal must be drawn. Open up the papers and laugh at the results.

Gossip Game: Everyone sits around in a close circle. Someone turns to his neighbor on the left and whispers a sentence. The neighbor whispers what he thinks he heard to the person on his left, and so on until it reaches the person who began it. Then he repeats what he has heard and tells what he originally said. You'll be amazed how garbled this whisper becomes after five or six repeats.

Gumdrop Race: Stretch a clothesline between two objects at least 6 feet apart. The line must be at least 6 or 8 inches over the heads of your guests. From this, suspend a line of gumdrops slightly higher than everyone's head. Blindfold all the players, and line them up before the gumdrop line. At the word "gumdrop," each contestant starts to eat gumdrops. The mighty eater who first gets three candies is the winner.

Identification: Players sit around a table, hands beneath it. You pass unseen objects one at a time — perhaps ten or twelve. Don't allow too much time between objects. When everything has been passed, have each guest make a list of what each object was.

Do the same with tasting. Blindfold each player and give him ten or twelve things to taste *once*. When everyone has had a chance, have them list what they tasted.

This can be done with things to smell as well.

Living Letters: Divide your guests into two teams. Each member of each team is given a letter, the teams having duplicate letters. Now you call out a word that can be spelled with those letters. The first team that spells the word correctly by lining up in the correct order wins. Then try to spell the word backwards. Marvelous confusion!

Magazine Game No. 1: Get one magazine for each guest. Go through each magazine before the party and make a list of ten items you found. Give each guest a magazine and the list of ten items for that magazine. Have everyone sit in circle, open their magazines, and search for and cut out the ten items on each list. The first one finished wins.

Magazine Game No. 2: Give each guest a magazine, scissors, paste or cellophane tape, and a large piece of blank paper. Tell each player to make his own picture by using parts of at least three separate pictures in the magazine, putting the pieces together so they will compose a picture. Funny or unusual pictures, rather than just pretty ones, are the object.

Make a Costume: Make up two teams. Give each team a 5-foot piece of brown wrapping paper, which you can purchase by the roll in any variety store. One member of each team lies down flat on the paper and his teammates trace the outline of his body. Each team is given crepe paper, paste, scissors, glitter dust, or anything else that could be used for decorating. The team works together to make a costume on the tracing. No winner — just the fun of doing.

Mod Art: This one requires imagination, too. Before the party, collect a variety of boxes in many shapes. They should be small, the kind that held such gifts as socks, ties, handkerchiefs, and so on. You'll need to provide scissors, crayons, and cellophane tape. Ask each person to make a mask, an animal, a boat, or anything he wants.

Observation: Each guest has a blank sheet of paper and a pencil. Have someone (why not you) come in wearing as many things as you can that can be seen. Make them odd, such as three neckties, a mark on your face, a half dozen rings, odd shoes, and so on. Walk around the room once and leave. Everyone has to list, in a given time, what you wore. Another version of this is to bring out a tray with twelve items on it — a can opener, a penny, a bobby pin, a fork, a rubber band, and so on. Place the tray in the center of the room and give everyone one minute to look. Take the tray away and ask everyone to list what they saw.

Pin the Nose On: This is the old pin-the-tail-on-the-donkey except that you make your own. Look through a magazine or newspaper and cut out the largest head you can find. Mount this on a poster board. When the game starts, just tape it to anything handy. Make a nose of cardboard, color it red, and fasten a thumbtack to it. Blindfold each guest, turn him around two or three times, head him in the right direction, and see where the nose ends up!

Playlets: The most complicated but most fun game of observation is to act out a little scene — a pretended murder, an accident, whatever you please. Beforehand you must prepare a number of questions (perhaps twenty or so) that relate to your playlet. For example, if it is a murder: What weapon was used? Did the victim carry

83

anything? Each guest will answer on paper as best he can. This will show you how few people make good witnesses.

Scrambled Words: Make a list of phrases that when placed together differently spell the name of a fruit. Example: Lo, men! (melon), No gear (orange), Eh, Cap? (peach), Great man, Poe (pomegranate). Leave a blank space beside each phrase so the guests may try their luck. This can be played with categories other than fruit — other foods, famous names, and so on.

Shaving Game: Choose couples — one customer, one barber. The barber is given a spoon and shaving cream to lather his customer's face. He then shaves his customer with the spoon. The first barber to complete the job is the winner — his customer wins, too.

Shorthand: Give each guest a list of definitions that can be answered with a *single* letter. About twenty-four definitions should be enough. Set a time limit and see who wins. Here are a few examples:

> A command to a horse (G)
> Not as large as an ocean (C)
> A spring vegetable (P)
> An insect (B)

Two-letter version:

> Cold (IC)
> A tent (TP)
> A vine (IV)
> A girl's name (LC)
> Not difficult (EZ)

Telegram: Each guest writes down ten letters as you call them off. Each player must write a ten-word telegram about a subject you choose, such as going on a trip or to a wedding. Each word must begin with the letters you called in the order you called them. For example: M, A, F, C, W, H, T, A, S, P. The telegram might be: Mother arriving from Cairo Wednesday Have taxi at station please.

Toss a Word: Seat all but one player in a semicircle. The standing player has a ball or a potato. He thinks of a noun such as automobile, and says the word as he tosses the ball to someone in the semicircle. This person must then say a word in direct relation to automobile, such as taxi, racer, convertible, sedan. The word must be specific. The player then tosses back the ball as he says the required word. If he misses, he becomes "it." Great fun and great confusion.

Word Game: Each person gets a piece of paper and a pencil. Take words like Halloween, Thanksgiving, Christmas, Valentine — any long word. Let everyone make as many words as possible from the letters of the chosen word.

6

Basic Skills

Skill 1. Making copies: Use regular carbon paper, cut to the size of your invitations. Place the decoration to be transferred in the most attractive position. Tape it lightly to the carbon paper so that it won't slip about as you work. It is best to tape the whole combination — blank paper to your work board, carbon to the blank paper, and the decoration to the carbon. If you have a very large area, piece together as many carbon sheets as is necessary to cover the area. Use the hidden seam method (Skill 3).

Skill 2. Compass: Take a square of paper a little larger than the size you want the circle to be. With a ruler, lightly draw a straight line from upper left-hand corner to lower right-hand corner. Then from upper right to lower left. Where the lines intersect is the center. Take a piece of string and tie one end around the shaft of a thumbtack and place the thumbtack in the center mark. Stretch the string from the center to one of the four sides (as indicated by the dotted line in the drawing). Allow ½-inch extra string, wrap it around your pencil, and tape it in place. You can make a compass any size you need.

Skill 3. Hidden seam: Along one edge of the seam to be hidden, place double-stick tape as shown. Starting with the ends equal, overlap the second piece of paper just enough to cover the tape and press down to make it adhere to the tape.

Skill 4. Enlarging: To enlarge a pattern, draw a rectangle or a square the size your finished object is to be. Everyone of the suggested drawings that you would enlarge in this book are done over ¼-inch squares. If you want a copy twice that size, mark off your paper in ½-inch squares. For three times the size of the drawing, make each square ¾ inch, and so on. Put into each square the shape or line that appears in the same square in the book. Be sure you don't make your squares with such heavy lines that they can't be erased from the finished product.

Skill 5. Crepe paper grain: You can see lines, or ridges, that run in the same direction all along the 20-inch width of the crepe paper. These lines are the "grain." If directions call for cutting across the grain, cut the paper at right angles to the lines. To cut with the grain means to cut in the same direction as the grain, or parallel to the lines.

Skill 6. Stretching crepe paper: It takes two people to do this. Wrap each end of the unfolded package around a yardstick or a broomstick two or three times. With each person holding an end, stretch gently until there is no more give. This is a good idea if you are making streamers or swags of crepe paper of any great length.

Skill 7. *Crushing crepe paper:* Do this any time you want a special effect. Stretch the paper (Skill 6), then wrap it around a broomstick, or if it is a small streamer, around any round object long enough to hold it. The grain of the paper should run parallel to the stick.

Skill 8. *Fringing crepe paper:* Cut across the grain to the desired width. Hold the thicknesses together with pins so they won't slip. For fringe, make a series of even cuts along one edge — the closer together the cuts, the finer the fringe. If you want pointed or petal shapes, make the cuts along the edge the desired distance apart, then round off or point the outer edge of each cut.

Skill 9. *Crepe ruffles:* Cut a strip of crepe paper across the grain twice the width of the ruffle needed. Fold the strip in half length-wise. Slip a knitting needle or ruler into the fold. Gather the paper onto the needle or ruler with the thumb and forefinger.

Skill 10. *Accordian fan flowers:* Use colored construction paper or any other paper in gay colors. If you want a 10-inch-diameter flower, cut 5 inches wide. Fold the paper into an accordian fold of ½-inch segments. Now fold this in half. Open and apply glue to the edges to be joined; press glued surfaces together. At the center of each fold put a dab of glue, then pinch together to form the fan. It is easier if you have a stapler — one staple does the trick. Make four of these and attach them together — a beautiful spot of color for your party.

Skill 11. *Fringed leaf flower:* Make three or four 5-inch circles, place them one on top of the other. Fold in half circles. Fold the half circle in half, making a quarter circle. Make 1-inch cuts about ⅛ inch apart around the entire outer edge. Unfold, and staple or sew the center of all the layers together. If you want a different colored center, cut two 1½-inch circles of your second color and repeat the above. Glue, staple, or sew to the center of the flower. Tape the flower to a wire hanger or hang on tape wherever you need color. Flowers can be made in any size, of course.

Skill 12. Fluting crepe paper: Stretch the edge of the crepe paper every ½ inch by holding it between the thumb and forefinger of each hand and bringing one hand toward you and pulling the other hand away from you.

Index